Chicago Tribune

A global pilgrim
The journeys of Pope John Paul II

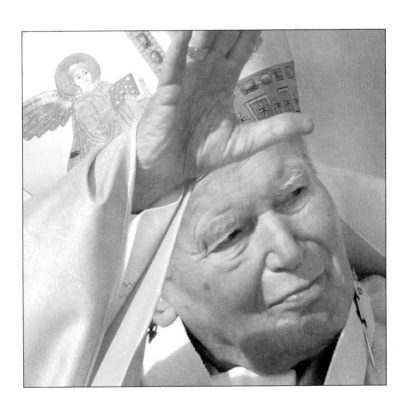

TRIUMPH
B O O K S
CHICAGO

Library of Congress Control Number: 2005901723

This book is available in quantity at special discounts for your group or organization. For further information, contact:

Triumph Books
601 South LaSalle Street
Suite 500
Chicago, Illinois 60605
(312) 939-3330
Fax (312) 663-3557

Printed in U.S.A.
ISBN-13: 978-1-57243-705-0
ISBN-10: 1-57243-705-7
Design by Eileen Wagner, Wagner/Donovan, Chicago, Illinois

Pope John Paul II, the most traveled pontiff in history, was greeted by enthusiastic multitudes—hundreds of thousands, even millions of people—in country after country over more than a quarter century. Some say he was seen in person by more people than anyone who ever lived.

Each of his journeys had a purpose. In some places, he emphasized the traditional stands of the church on issues such as abortion, women in the clergy and the evils of materialism. Some would say bravely while others would say stubbornly, he brought those positions to the very audiences who least wanted to hear them. He traveled to confront communism that ruled his native Poland—and, through his visits, helped end its grip. He spoke out against unbridled capitalism, dehumanizing globalism and rampant consumerism.

His long global odyssey seemed, in a way, a series of family visits, calling on the world's 1 billion Roman Catholics. In historic journeys to mend centuries-old estrangements, he also reached out to members of other faiths.

The photos documenting his travels include strikingly similar images: huge crowds of people reaching out to touch him, a reaction perhaps to having been so deeply touched by him. Though the faces change across racial and ethnic boundaries—Polish-Americans in Chicago, colorfully dressed Nigerians, young girls in Portugal, Cubans gathered in Havana's Revolution Plaza—their expressions of faith and hope remain remarkably the same.

The family he touched was humanity. ▨

Czestochowa, Poland, 1979

The holy shrine at
Fatima, Portugal, 2000

Airport at Yaoundé, capital of Cameroon, 1995

As was his custom, kissing the ground upon landing, here at Auckland, New Zealand, 1986

CONTENTS

Maribor, Slovenia, 1999

From Wadowice to the Vatican

Most people who grew up in the small, ancient town of Wadowice in southern Poland didn't venture far from the area. But Karol Wojtyla (voy-TIH-wah), born there May 18, 1920, to Karol Wojtyla, an administrative officer in the Polish army, and his wife, former schoolteacher Emilia Kaczorowska Wojtyla, would become famed for his travels.

As Pope John Paul II, the bishop of Rome, vicar of Christ, successor of St. Peter, supreme pastor of the Roman Catholic Church, Wojtyla jetted around the world, traveling with a pilgrim's determination and evangelist's fervor that, in his old age, overcame increasing infirmity.

Wojtyla's mother wanted the boy she called "Lolek" to become a priest, and assembled a small altar for his room. She had been sickly all her life and died after a prolonged stay in bed when Karol was 8. A teacher in his school gave him the news.

"It was God's will," the boy said.

Three years later, his older brother, Edmund, a physician, caught scarlet fever from a patient and died.

Karol and his father lived in a second floor apartment in a stone house at 7 Koscielna St., and took their main meals in a nearby bar and cafe. The senior Wojtyla devoted himself to raising the boy with the sort of military discipline that had shaped his own life. Trained as a tailor, he made clothing for Karol from old uniforms. He crafted a soccer ball from rags. He taught him German (with an Austrian accent) and instilled a love for Polish literature.

Father and son attended mass together each morning, and often went on evening walks. The pope would recall life with his devoutly religious father as a sort of "domestic seminary."

He attended a state-run boys school that offered a classical education with Latin and Greek at its core. He joined the Sodality of Mary, a society fostering devotion to the mother of Christ. He attended a mandatory cadet camp and studied military preparedness. He became ever more immersed in

Karol with his mother, Emilia

Wojtyla, as a priest, on an outing with a Catholic youth group

Wadowice's school-based theater, and it was thought around town that the stage would be his calling.

As a teen, Karol, already a fine student, became an athlete. He was a soccer goalie. He swam in rivers flooded by spring snowmelts. He hiked in the nearby mountains, and, in the winter, skied them with devil-may-care abandon. He liked to kayak, and later as a priest, he'd go along on campouts with young people, sometimes offering mass using an overturned kayak as an altar and two oars strapped together as a cross.

He graduated from secondary school as valedictorian in 1938 and moved with his father to nearby Krakow, the intellectual and cultural center of the nation. There he enrolled in the Jagiellonian University to study literature and philosophy. He joined an experimental theater group and was a talented actor. He sang well and wrote poetry.

Among his college poems was one recalling his mother's death. It began, "Oh, how many years have gone by without you ..."

On Sept. 1, 1939, Germany invaded Poland. Wojtyla was in the Krakow cathedral that morning and heard the warning sirens, and then the barking of anti-aircraft guns and the explosions of bombs dropped by Luftwaffe aircraft. As fighter planes strafed the outskirts of town, he ran for home and

into a six-year-long hell. He later recalled the Nazi occupation as a time of "fear, violence, extreme poverty, death, tragic experiences of painful separation, endured in the absence of all security and freedom; recurring traumas brought about by the incessant bloodshed."

Some of his Jewish friends, aware of what was happening in Germany, already had fled Poland. He would lose many more to the death camps, including nearby Auschwitz.

In order to obtain a work permit and avoid imprisonment or even execution, Wojtyla became a laborer and worked in a limestone quarry.

The clergy went underground in a less literal way as Nazi occupiers continued to strip Poland of its priests as well as its Jews and intellectuals. Services were offered at locations revealed only at the last minute. Wojtyla refused to be intimidated; his faith grew under the harsh repression, and he led one cell of a clandestine Catholic youth group.

In 1941, his father died of a heart attack.

"After my father's death," he told a biographer, "I gradually became aware of my true path." He said his vocation became "an inner fact of unquestionable and absolute clarity. The following year, in the autumn, I knew that I was called."

A secret seminary was established hidden within a church building in Krakow. Ten candidates

Left and above: A 19-year-old Wojtyla, center, in a Polish military training camp, Eastern Poland, 1939

were selected to be the first class of priests to attend. Wojtyla was among them. In 1946, in the private chapel of the archbishop of Krakow, he was ordained a priest, the formal beginning of his relatively speedy path to the papacy.

His first assignment was a test of his adaptability and resolve. He was sent to Niegowic, a desperately poor, undeveloped, rural parish east of Krakow. Seven months later, having risen to that challenge, he was assigned to a thriving parish in Krakow, St. Florian's, a church of choice for university students.

As time passed, the Catholic Church again came under attack—this time by the Soviets. In 1951, his archbishop advised Wojtyla to take a leave from priestly duties, go to Rome and earn

another degree, thus protecting him for future service to God.

In 1958, a vacancy opened for a new auxiliary bishop in Krakow. Wojtyla was approved for the post and consecrated that same year.

The next year, Pope John XXIII announced plans for the Second Vatican Council, which would convene four times between 1962 and 1965. The archbishop of Krakow had just died, and Wojtyla became the temporary head of the archdiocese, gaining him a seat at the defining event of the Catholic Church in the 20th Century.

When it was time to appoint a new archbishop in Krakow, communist officials turned down the first two lists of candidates. Wojtyla, seen as an academic, intellectual and poet rather than a political threat, was accepted. He was appointed in January 1964.

Three years later, having impressed Pope Paul VI with his post-Vatican II writings and his work on the pope's commission on birth control, Wojtyla was elevated to cardinal.

In 1978, after just four ballots, Cardinal Albino Luciani, patriarch of Venice, became Pope John Paul I. Thirty-three days later, he died.

It would have been axiomatic that an Italian would be chosen—as had been the case for more than 400 years—but two Italian factions formed with a sharp split between them. More and more, Cardinal Wojtyla was mentioned. He was, at 58, very young to be pope, but he had brought life and

Above: As a young priest, with first communicants
Right: Visiting the Parthenon as a bishop,
Athens, 1963

growth to the Polish church under communist repression. Perhaps he could reinvigorate the church as a whole.

On Oct. 16, 1978, the College of Cardinals chose Wojtyla, and he, honoring his predecessors, chose the name John Paul II. The news was announced from a balcony overlooking St. Peter's Square.

Someone in the crowd spoke for most of them, "Un papa straniero!" "a foreign pope!"

When he stepped out to address the people, John Paul II immediately and charmingly defused any concern.

"I am your new bishop of Rome, called from a distant country," he said. "I don't know if I can make myself clear in your—our Italian language. If I make a mistake, you will correct me."

This was said, of course, in perfect Italian. ▪

Charles Leroux
Tribune senior correspondent

CLEMENS·X·PONT·MAX·
ANNO·IVBILEI·MDCLXXV·

In a ceremony
to seal the
Holy Door of
St. Peter's
Basilica, 2001

Chapter 1

Latin America: The pilgrimage begins

In 1979, not long after being installed as pope, John Paul II made his first papal trip abroad, to Latin America. While praying in Mexico City before an image of the Virgin Mary, he had an epiphany that would shape the long pontificate that lay before him.

He saw that he would become a pilgrim with the whole world as his destination. He would tour the globe much as a parish priest might tour his parish. Like that priest, he would inspire and comfort and teach and admonish. He would do this not just as head of the church speaking remotely from the Vatican, but as the church's living, breathing manifestation, a physical presence at the eye of the storm of attention that surrounded him.

It was one thing to issue a statement chastising some of the Latin American clergy for their political activism, but the message came simpler and stronger when the pope stood in front of a Nicaraguan priest and shook his finger in the man's face. His thoughts on the inhumanity of the exploitation of laborers had real muscle when delivered amid thousands of poor, indigenous people in Cuilapam de Guerrero, Mexico.

"The pope wants to be your voice," he told them, "the voice of those who cannot speak or are silent; the defender of the oppressed, who have the right to effective help, not charity or the crumbs of justice." ▪

Cuilapam
de Guerrero,
Mexico, 1979

Puebla, Mexico, 1979

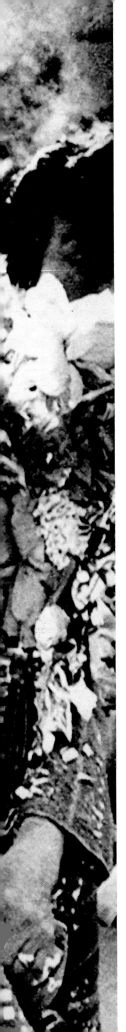

Above: Rio de Janeiro, 1997
Left: Puebla, Mexico, 1979
Facing page: Cakchiqueles
tribespeople, Guatemala City, 1983

Left: Passing the Che Guevara mural
Below: Mass in Sacred Heart Church, Havana
Facing page: Greeted by President Fidel Castro on the pope's only visit to Cuba, José Martí Airport, Havana, 1998

Chapter 2

Poland: Breaking the grip of communism

Born in southern Poland near Krakow, Karol Wojtyla grew to be a priest, of course, but he also was an actor, hiker, playwright, kayaker, philosopher and—during Nazi occupation and, later, communist rule—a witness to evil.

Wojtyla had friends in Krakow's Jewish community, which was nearly obliterated when Nazis murdered many of its people outright and sent others to the death camp at nearby Auschwitz. For this pope, revulsion toward anti-Semitism was personal.

He was the first pope to have lived under communism, a system he felt robbed people of their humanity. When he was elected, the Poles felt a tremendous psychological lift. The pope, however, would prove to be more than just a symbolic ally.

On his first visit home as pope in 1979, he laid the intellectual foundation for the labor movement Solidarity. On his second visit in 1983, John Paul II confronted his reluctant host, Gen. Wojciech Jaruzelski, Poland's leader. With the pope's support, the Polish people forced one of the first cracks in Soviet communism.

Jaruzelski seemed shaky when he greeted the pope. He said he was nervous because his prepared speech had not yet arrived. Others in his regime later said it was because he realized the pope's message of human dignity carried inexorable power. He saw the pontiff's visit as the beginning of the end. ■

First visit to his homeland as pope, Warsaw military airport, 1979

Warsaw's Victory Square cleared for
helicopter arrival, 1979

Above: Meeting with an uneasy Polish Gen. Wojciech Jaruzelski in Krakow, 1983
Facing page, top: Solidarity demonstration after a service held by the pope in Krakow, 1983
Bottom: Poland under martial law imposed to prevent Solidarity from gaining power, Warsaw, 1982

Above: Visiting his parents' and older brother's graves at Rakowicki
cemetery in Krakow, 2002
Facing page: Surprise visit to members of the Milewski family, farmers in
the village of Leszczewo in northeast Poland, 1999

Krakow, 2002

Chapter 3

The Middle East: Patching old wounds

In a centuries-old ritual, Jews insert messages written on small pieces of paper into cracks in Jerusalem's Western Wall. During his millennium-year visit to the Holy Land, John Paul II joined in this tradition to give a historic message to the Jewish people.

Without specifically fixing blame, his note asked forgiveness for the suffering Jews had endured over the years. In it, he pledged to "commit ourselves to genuine brotherhood with the people of the covenant." It was a landmark moment in a career of outreach.

He was the first pope ever to set foot in the main synagogue in Rome, home to the city's 2,000-year-old Jewish community. He was the first pope to enter a mosque. He met with Sunni Muslim clerics in Cairo. At the foot of Mt. Sinai, he entered a 6th Century Greek Orthodox monastery, a step toward mending an estrangement 1,000 or more years old.

He said that Roman Catholicism had developed the rational aspect of the faith while Orthodoxy had embraced the mystic, and that each needed the other. His had been an influential voice in the Second Vatican Council, which had called for Eastern and Western faiths to join so that the church could "breathe with two lungs."

The pope was able to encompass seeming contradictions. While playing up the similarities of various faiths, he also underscored the uniqueness of Catholicism by emphasizing the Virgin Mary and insisting that clergy wear priestly garb to set them apart from the secular world. ▪

God of our fathers,
you chose Abraham and his descendants
to bring your Name to the Nations:
we are deeply saddened
by the behaviour of those
who in the course of history
have caused these children of yours to suffer,
and asking your forgiveness
we wish to commit ourselves
to genuine brotherhood
with the people of the Covenant.

Jerusalem, 26 March 2000

Joannes Paulus II

Pilgrims waving Palestinian, Vatican, Israeli and Lebanese flags before a papal mass by the Sea of Galilee, Israel, 2000

Above: At the residence of Sunni Muslim leader Sheik Mohammed
Sayed Tantawi (third from left), Cairo, 2000
Facing page: St. Catherine's Greek Orthodox Monastery, where Moses is
said to have received the 10 Commandments, Mt. Sinai, Egypt, 2000

Jerusalem's Western
Wall, 2000

Chapter 4

North America: Stranger in a strange land

In 1979, on his first papal visit to North America, John Paul II stood before 75,000 people in Yankee Stadium in New York City, the city where, if you "can make it there, you can make it anywhere." There, of all places, he decried the excesses of materialism.

He said Christians must make "a decisive break with the frenzy of consumerism, exhausting and joyless. It is not a question of slowing down progress, for there is no human progress when everything conspires to give full rein to self interest, sex and power."

By emphasizing the traditional values of Catholicism, including stands against divorce and the sexual revolution, he was challenging what seemed to him the rapid erosion of morality throughout the modern world. Nowhere was that erosion seen more clearly than in the U.S.

Despite his countercultural stance, he was greeted like a celebrity. Time magazine called him "John Paul, Superstar." When he came to Madison Square Garden to tell tens of thousands of teenagers to accept moral responsibility for their lives, a school band played the theme from the popular movie "Rocky."

Some Americans might have ignored his message or been made uncomfortable by it, but most found this pope personally irresistible. At that gathering of teens, when the crowd chanted, "John Paul II, we love you," he answered, "John Paul II, he loves you." ■

Popemobile on overpass,
Los Angeles, 1987

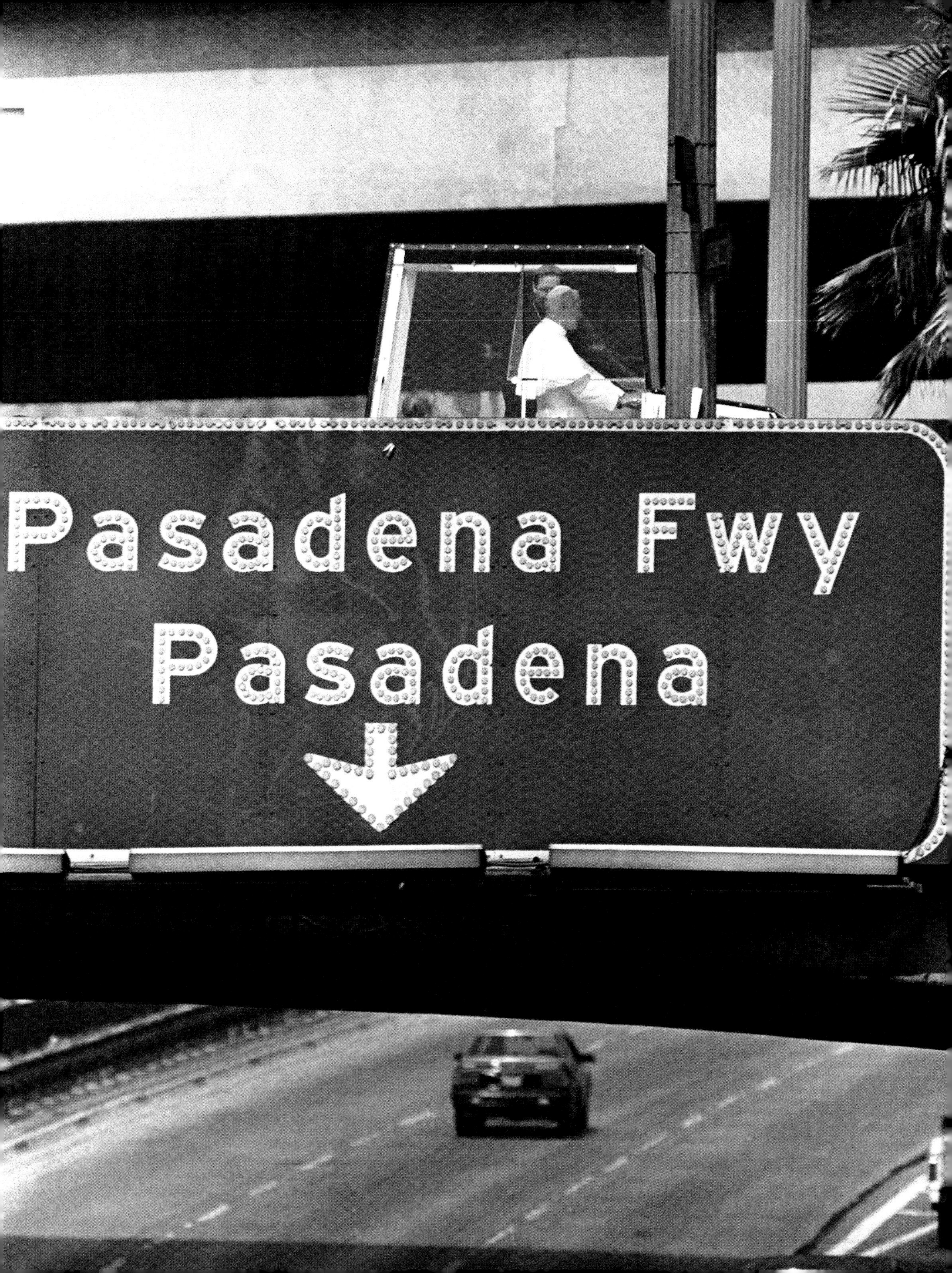
Pasadena Fwy
Pasadena

Papal mass, Boston, 1979

Above: Los Angeles, 1987
Left: Grant Park mass, Chicago, 1979
Facing page, top: Souvenirs, San Antonio, 1987
Facing page, bottom: Chicago, 1979

Above: Preaching abstinence from drugs and sex to young people, New Orleans' Superdome, 1987
Facing page: Pima tribe purification ceremony, Phoenix, 1987

Sharing the TV lights with President
Ronald Reagan, Miami, 1987

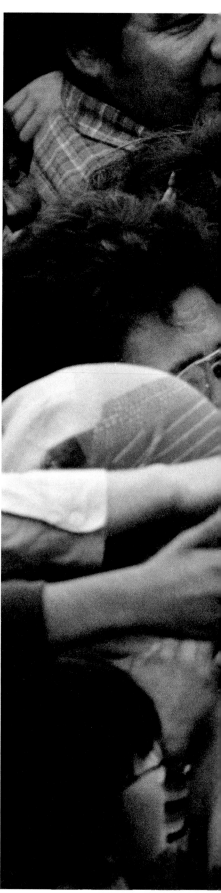

Above: Embracing a 5-year-old AIDS
patient, San Francisco, 1987
Facing page: St. Anne de Beaupre,
Quebec, 1984

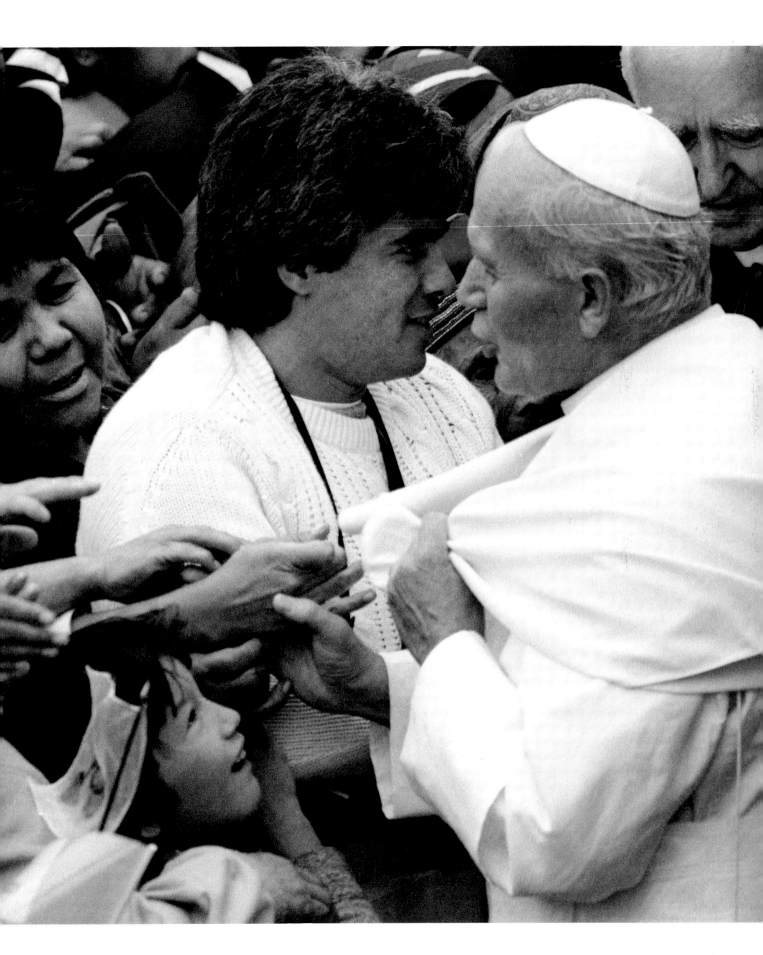

Saying the rosary while
walking through the woods,
Elk Island National Park,
Alberta, 1984

Above: Windy day in the LeBreton Flats area of Ottawa, 1984
Facing page: World Youth Day, Downsview Park, Toronto, 2002

Twilight, Quebec City, 1984

WE LOVE YOU

POPE JOHN PAUL II

Chicago, 1979

Holy Name Cathedral, Chicago, 1979

Chapter 5

The globe: Touching humanity one soul at a time

For years, each time John Paul II reached his destination and got off the plane, he knelt and kissed the ground, emphasizing that every place on Earth is sacred, that the planet we all share is holy ground. Later, when age and illness made him unsteady, a small container of soil would be brought to him and lifted to his lips.

Often, when he would face millions, news reports would talk of "speaking to the masses." He never thought of it that way. To him, those seas of upturned faces were millions of unique souls, each posing a question for which the answer was Christ.

He spoke the languages of most who came to him. In addition to the Latin used in the mass, the pope was fluent in Polish, English, Italian, Spanish, German, Lithuanian and French and, when necessary, learned phrases of languages outside his grasp.

Not that everyone who understood his words agreed with them. His unyielding stands on controversial issues sometimes made him the target of protest. On a visit to Germany, for instance, his popemobile was spattered with red paint.

In an era of mass communication, he understood globally what a candidate for councilman understood locally: the power of personal appearance. Anyone who ever stood on tiptoes in a throng of people just to get a glimpse of him tells later of when "I saw the pope."

In flight during a tour
of the U.S., 1987

Mother Teresa, Calcutta, India, 1986

Top: Bosnia, 1997
Above: Blessing of the sick and elderly, St. Martin's Basilica, Tours, France, 1996
Facing page: Vehicle window smeared with paint by a protester, Berlin, 1996

QUE SOY
ERA
IMMACULADA COUNCEPCIOU

The grotto where, in 1858, the Virgin Mary is said to have appeared to Bernadette Soubirou, Lourdes, France, 2004

Chapter 1

The pontiff

When the head of the world's largest church was not on the road, John Paul II, the 264th bishop of Rome, was surrounded by the marble floors, the Renaissance paintings, the Swiss Guards, the baroque grandeur of the Vatican, his command center, his office, his home.

Early on, he made it clear to his staff that he would set the tone for his pontificate. He told security people to step aside so he could wade into crowds to touch and be touched. He insisted on referring to himself as "I" or "me" rather than the royal "we" most popes had used.

He did most of his writing in the Vatican. He was a prolific producer of encyclicals, apostolic exhortations, constitutions, letters and other documents, often writing for hours in longhand. Beyond his church writings, he produced several popular books and participated in CDs containing songs, prayers and speeches.

He also was prolific in proclaiming saints, canonizing and beatifying far more than all previous popes together. It was part of his global view, an effort to show that saints are not just part of a long-ago Europe, but could appear anywhere on Earth, especially in response to the challenges of the modern world.

The first non-Italian pope in more than four centuries made the Vatican his as he, sometimes controversially, sometimes historically, shaped the church. He visited the world as the pilgrim pope. In Rome, the world came to him. ▦

Inaugurating the restored
Sistine Chapel, 1999

Pilgrims from Chicago
gathering for a photo with
the Holy Father, 2003

Above: Lights in the top floor windows from the papal apartments
overlooking St. Peter's Square, 2003
Facing page: In his private chapel, praying for the victims of the
terrorist bomb attack in Madrid, 2004

Chapter 2

The victim

It was common to see hands rising from the crowds as John Paul II passed, hands waving, hands holding cameras, hands reaching out to him. But one spring day in May 1981, as his jeep passed through St. Peter's Square, one hand rising above the throng held a pistol.

Two shots were fired. One bullet grazed him, but the other hit a hand and ricocheted, tearing through his abdomen, "miraculously" (one of the doctors said) missing his vital organs.

Shortly after regaining consciousness, the pope forgave his assailant, Mehmet Ali Agca, an escaped Turkish murderer. After recuperation, John Paul II appeared in the square where he had been shot and thanked God for permitting him "to experience suffering, and the danger of losing my life."

Later he visited Agca in prison. Their conversation was never revealed, but, at one point, Agca bent to kiss the pope's hand. Sitting with the man who had tried to kill him gave flesh and blood and breath to the virtue of forgiveness the pope long had espoused.

Just nine months after the attack, he was back in the air, heading for Africa, more determined than ever to pursue his pilgrimage. ▦

Gunman in the crowd to the left moments before
shots were fired, St. Peter's Square

Above: With his assailant, Mehmet Ali Agca, in Rebibbia prison, Rome, 1983
Facing page: Wounded, slumping in his vehicle

Chapter 3

The priest

Each year, during the week leading up to Easter, the pinnacle of the Christian calendar, John Paul II led services commemorating the death and resurrection of Christ. The week builds to the Triduum (Latin for "three days") that begins with the consecration of the Eucharist on the evening of Holy Thursday. It continues with the Stations of the Cross at the Roman Colosseum on Good Friday, the midnight Easter vigil, and culminates with evening prayers on Easter Sunday.

During the 2003 Easter service, John Paul II called for an end "to the chain of hatred and terrorism, which threatens the orderly development of the human family. May God grant that we be free from the peril of a tragic clash between cultures and religions. May faith and love of God make the followers of every religion courageous builders of understanding and forgiveness, patient weavers of a fruitful interreligious dialogue, capable of inaugurating a new era of justice and peace."

Dome of St. Peter's

Evening service in St. Peter's Basilica

Above: Crowding St. Peter's Square,
Easter Sunday, 2003
Right: The Swiss Guards
Facing page: The faithful undeterred
by on-and-off rain

Arriving to celebrate Easter mass, 2003

John Paul II

1920 - 2005

Chicago Tribune

Publisher
David Hiller

Editor
Ann Marie Lipinski

Managing editor
James O'Shea

A global pilgrim
THE JOURNEYS OF POPE JOHN PAUL II

Photo editor
José Moré

Editors
Steve Kloehn
Charles Leroux
Jill Boba

Imagers
Don Bierman
Christine Bruno
Kathy Celer

Project managers
Tony Majeri
Bill Parker
Susan Zukrow

Designer
Eileen Wagner,
Wagner/Donovan Design

Photo credits

COVER
Patrick Hertzog/AFP/Getty: front cover
Anne Cusack/Chicago Tribune: back cover

INTRODUCTION
Patrick Hertzog/AFP/Getty: title page
AP: 2-3
Paolo Cocco/Reuters: 4-5
Jean-Marc Bouju/AP: 6-7
Jean-Claude Delmas/AFP/Getty: 8-9
Gabriel Bouys/AFP/Getty: 10-11

BOOK 1
Archive of "The Family Home of John Paul II": 13
Chicago Tribune files: 14, 16 (top)
AP: 15
Catholic News Service: 16 (bottom)
Arturo Mari/AP: 17

BOOK 2
CHAPTER 1: LATIN AMERICA
José Moré/UPI: 19
Anne Cusack/Chicago Tribune: 20-21, 23 (bottom)
Pete Leabo/AP: 22
Arturo Mari/AP: 23 (top)
José Moré/Chicago Tribune: 24-25

CHAPTER 2: POLAND
UPI: 27
Hugo Peralta/UPI: 28-29, 30 (top)
AP: 30 (bottom)
AP/Interpress: 31
Vatican: 32
Pier Paolo Cito/AP: 33
Vincenzo Pinto/AP: 34-35

CHAPTER 3: THE MIDDLE EAST
Jim Hollander/Reuters: 37
Francois Guillot/AFP/Getty: 38-39
Arturo Mari/AP: 40
Amr Nabil/AP: 41
Gabriel Bouys/Reuters: 42-43

CHAPTER 4: NORTH AMERICA
Chris Walker/Chicago Tribune: 45, 48 (top), 49 (top)
Bob Fila/Chicago Tribune: 46-47, 49 (bottom), 63
Ernie Cox Jr./Chicago Tribune: 48 (bottom)
José Moré/Chicago Tribune: 50-51, 54-55, 58, 60-61
Pete Souza/White House: 52-53
Vatican: 56-57
Kevin Frayer/AP: 59
Charles Osgood/Chicago Tribune: 62
Bob Fila/Chicago Tribune: 63

CHAPTER 5: THE GLOBE
Daniel Goodrich/Newsday: 65
AP: 66-67
Charles Osgood/Chicago Tribune: 68 (top)
Peter Dejong/AP: 68 (bottom)
Gero Breloer/AFP/DPA: 69
Splash News: 70-71

BOOK 3
CHAPTER 1: THE PONTIFF
Paolo Cocco/Reuters: 73
José Moré/Chicago Tribune: 74-75, 77
Reuters: 76

CHAPTER 2: THE VICTIM
AP: 79-81
Tommy Anderson/AP: 82
Arturo Mari/AP: 83

CHAPTER 3: THE PRIEST
José Moré/Chicago Tribune: 85-93